SHAKESPEARE IN SHORTS

A Play in One Act

LICENSING & PRODUCTION INQUIRIES
Uproar Theatrics, LLC.
hello@uproartheatrics.com | www.UproarTheatrics.com

Shakespeare in Shorts copyright © 2025 by David Overton

Shakespeare in Shorts is published by Uproar Theatrics, LLC
500 8th Ave FRNT 3, #1714 New York, NY 10018

ISBN: 978-1-968051-08-2

First Printing, May 2025

Playwright's Note

SHAKESPEARE IN SHORTS is intended to edify, enlighten and entertain an audience (and the young performers themselves) about the works and life of William Shakespeare.

The set is minimal and flexible (levels created by cubes or risers can be sufficient).

The fast-paced comedy and banter require mastery of dialogue and precision in movement.

All performers should wear shorts. Costume pieces (capes, crowns, royal staff) can be added to supplement a character for clarity.

For the majority of the play, the performers speak directly to the audience. There are opportunities for doubling and even tripling as suits the needs of the production. Pronouns within the text should be changed when, where, and as needed, no additional approval from Uproar necessary.

Flexible, gender-blind casting for as many as 23 actors (with the exception of ACTOR A who should be female); or, by reducing the number of NARRATORS from 9 to 3 – and using the same actors in all of the Shakespearean scenes – as few as 11.

The playwright has given his permission for licensees to cut lines and/or scenes as necessary to meet the festival or competition's time requirements without seeking prior approval from Uproar. Lines must still be performed sequentially as written, and words may not be changed or substituted without prior written approval.

Cast of Characters

NARRATOR A
NARRATOR B
NARRATOR C
NARRATOR D
NARRATOR E
NARRATOR F
NARRATOR G
NARRATOR H
NARRATOR J
ACTOR A (female)
ACTOR B
ACTOR C
ROMEO
JULIET
HAMLET
OPHELIA
CLAUDIUS
GERTRUDE
OSRIC
LAERTES
HORATIO
PROSPERO
ARIEL

SETTING: *Bare stage with, perhaps, a few levels. Everyone starts onstage sitting in groups strategically arranged by the director except* NARRATORS A, B *and* C *who are standing center, facing upstage. Lights up.* NARRATORS A, B, C *simultaneously turn to face audience.*

NARRATOR A, B and C
(*prolong the "a" in "ladies" to get the audience's attention*)
Laaaaaaaaadies and Gentlemen!

NARRATOR A
Mesdames et Messieurs!

NARRATOR B
Moms and dads!

NARRATOR C
Sisters and brothers!

NARRATOR A
Teachers and administrators!

NARRATOR B
Friends, Romans, countrymen!

NARRATOR C
(*measured, with gravitas*) Lend. Me. Your. Ears!

NARRATOR A
(*beat, then with gusto*) And welcome to our Ted Talk on, Shakespeare's plays!

NARRATOR B
This isn't Ted Talk.

NARRATOR C

Shhhh!

NARRATOR B
(*quietly*) We could get sued.

NARRATOR C
(*quietly*) Go with it.

NARRATOR A
Theatre has been practiced for many, many years.

NARRATOR B
In many different forms.

NARRATOR C
In many different places.

NARRATOR B
In many different languages.

NARRATOR C
In many different –

NARRATOR A
That's enough with the different-ces!

NARRATOR C
All right, all right.

NARRATOR A
And came down to us – theatre, that is – from our fathers!

NARRATOR C
And our father's fathers!

NARRATOR A
Yes, we get it.

NARRATOR B
And from our father's, father's fathers!

NARRATOR A
Stop it, now!

NARRATOR B
Just trying to be comprehensive.

NARRATOR A
The Greeks gave us our first tragedies.

ALL
Ooooh…

NARRATOR C
And comedies!

ALL
Aaaaah…

NARRATOR
 Which gave rise to Roman comedies (ALL *give a quick laugh and motion*).

NARRATOR C
And tragedies (ALL *give a quick 'death' sound and motion*).

NARRATOR A
Which were largely based on Greek tragedies and comedies.

NARRATOR B
In fact, the Romans borrowed many ideas and philosophies from the Greeks.

NARRATOR C

Including their gods.

NARRATOR B

Including their gods.

NARRATOR

Which is why that for virtually every Roman god there is a Greek equivalent.

NARRATOR B

And predecessor.

NARRATOR C

Goes without saying.

NARRATOR A

After the fall of Rome,

ALL

(*descending, tragic*) Duh, duh, duh, duuuuhhh!

NARRATOR B

Things in Europe became rather bleak and dark for performance.

NARRATOR C

(*raises hand*) Is that why they are called the "Dark Ages"?

NARRATOR A

No. (*quickly*) As I was saying, after the fall of Rome, things became rather bleak and dark for performance *until* the Church began using aspects of theatre for instruction.

NARRATOR C

You see, the language of the Church and scholars in the European West was Latin,

NARRATOR B

And the language of the common people was, well,

NARRATOR C

Not…Latin.

NARRATOR A

It was whatever language the common person spoke in everyday situations.

NARRATOR B

Scholars refer to it as the 'vernacular.'

NARRATOR A

That's a big word.

NARRATOR B

Thank you. Oh, and if you don't know what 'vernacular' means, try Google.

NARRATOR A

Most people were illiterate.

NARRATOR B

They couldn't read.

NARRATOR A

That's what I just said.

NARRATOR B

No, you didn't. You said they were 'illiterate.'

NARRATOR A

That's what illiterate means; means they can't read.

NARRATOR B

Oh. Right.

NARRATOR A

And so, the Church would hold performances so that –

NARRATOR B

Wait, wait. So, do you mean 'illiterate' as in, 'they know how to read, they just don't do it?' Or 'they don't know how to read because they never learnt how to?'

NARRATOR A

(*slowly, as if talking to a child*) I mean, they were illiterate as in 'they don't read because they never learnt how to read.'

NARRATOR B

(*prolonged*) Oooooooh!

NARRATOR C

How did you get a part in this show?

NARRATOR B

(*shrugs shoulders*) I know the director.

NARRATOR A

So, the Church would hold performances of the stories of the Bible in an effort to educate the masses about the teachings of the Church.

NARRATOR B

Sounds very useful.

NARRATOR A

It was.

NARRATOR B

How long did this go on?

NARRATOR C

Glad you asked. Allow them (NARRATOR D, E, *and* F *step forward*).

NARRATOR D, E, F

Allow us!

NARRATOR F

We're much like them.

NARRATOR E

Only different.

NARRATOR C

See? More different-ces!

NARRATOR D

We are here to explain...

NARRATOR E

...the historical background...

NARRATOR F

...of how Shakespeare was able to flourish...

NARRATOR D, E, F

...as a playwright!

NARRATOR E

And while describing these events, select performers from our corps of ... (*realizes they will have to repeat the word 'performers'*) performers will enact said events through pantomime and interpretive dance.

> *During the following section, the historical figures mentioned might be enacted as follows:*

GERTRUDE *is Queen Elizabeth I,* OPHELIA *is Mary I,* CLAUDIUS *is Henry VIII,* ARIEL *is Anne Boleyn,* JULIET *is Catherine of Aragon,* ACTOR A *is Jane Seymour, and* HORATIO *is Edward VI. These assignments are interchangeable. The movement should suit what is being described and can be modified based upon the performers' abilities. It is all improvised and might change from performance to performance unless the director prefers to 'set' the action. The movement described is but broad strokes of what should be created. It is up to the performers and directors to develop the pantomime and dance.* NARRATOR D, E, F *move to the periphery.* GERTRUDE, OPHELIA, CLAUDIUS, ARIEL, JULIET, ACTOR A, HORATIO – *as there aforementioned characters – crouch in a semi-circle ready to spring into action.*

NARRATOR F

Around 1558, Queen Elizabeth I issued an edict which stated that there would be no more religious dramas.

GERTRUDE (*as* ELIZABETH I) *scribbles in the air, moves to the side.*

NARRATOR E

Why didn't she want religious dramas?

NARRATOR F

They were causing a lot of trouble.

NARRATOR D

You see, Elizabeth I had come to the throne just after her elder, half-sister, Mary I was queen.

>OPHELIA (*as* MARY I) *steps forward, stern in expression.*

NARRATOR E

She…

NARRATOR D

(*interjects name for clarity*) Mary…

NARRATOR E

…had tried to turn England back to the Catholic Church after her father -

NARRATOR F

Henry VIII,

>CLAUDIUS (*as* HENRY VIII) *steps forward, he is larger than life, waves his hand in English fashion.*

NARRATOR E

…had broken with the Catholic Church…

NARRATOR F

…because he wanted to marry Anne Boleyn.

>ARIEL (*as* ANNE BOLEYN) *steps forward, coy but alluring.*

NARRATOR D

Well, yes. But it was a little more complicated than that.

NARRATOR F

But let's try and piece it together. Ready?

NARRATOR D
No.

NARRATOR E
(*more excitedly than* NARRATOR D's *remark*) Yes!

NARRATOR F
You start.

NARRATOR E
So, Mary I's father,

NARRATOR F
Henry VIII,

NARRATOR E
Had broken with the Catholic Church, divorced his first wife,

NARRATOR D
Catherine of Aragon

> *CLAUDIUS (as HENRY VIII) pushes JULIET (as CATHERINE OF ARAGON) aside.*

NARRATOR F
…of Spain,

NARRATOR D
But not before they had a daughter, who would later become Mary I,

NARRATOR E
…then Henry VIII married Anne Boleyn,

NARRATOR D
…of England who had fiery, red hair,

NARRATOR E

…had her beheaded,

> CLAUDIUS (*as* HENRY VIII) *makes a slashing movement across* ARIEL'S *neck.* ARIEL (*as* ANNE BOLEYN) *is dragged away by* NARRATOR A.

NARRATOR F

But not before they had a daughter, who would later become Elizabeth I,

NARRATOR E

Then he married Jane Seymour,

> ACTOR A (*as* JANE SEYMOUR) *steps forward. Her attitude is one of duty and obedience.*

NARRATOR D

Of England, but she would die after giving birth to their son,

NARRATOR F

…who would later become Edward VI,

HORATIO (*as* EDWARD VI) *steps forward, gives peace sign.*

NARRATOR E

But now that we're clear on how we got to Henry VIII's third child…

NARRATOR D

…and only son,

NARRATOR D, E, F
Edward VI,

NARRATOR F
We can go back and explain how with each monarch after Henry VIII's death, the religious makeup of England became –

NARRATOR D, E, F
complicated.

NARRATOR D
But before we get to that, we should explain that Henry VIII married three more times –

NARRATOR F
For a total of six marriages,

NARRATOR E
But none of the last three wives have any bearing on Shakespeare.

NARRATOR D
This is a play about Shakespeare, after all.

NARRATOR F
It is?

NARRATOR D
It is.

NARRATOR F
I'd almost forgotten.

NARRATOR E
Keep up. Now then, Henry VIII was initially Catholic.

NARRATOR D, E, F
(*muttering, crossing themselves Catholic style*) In the name
of the father, the son, and the holy spirit, amen.

NARRATOR D
As we mentioned earlier.

NARRATOR E
When he broke with the Catholic Church, he began to
establish a Protestant or Anglican Church.

NARRATOR F
Which did not pledge any allegiance to the Pope in Rome.

NARRATOR D
After Henry VIII died, he appointed his youngest child,

NARRATOR E, F
Edward VI…

NARRATOR D
…to be his successor.

HORATIO (*as* EDWARD VI) *steps forward,
makes peace sign.*

NARRATOR E
And so, Edward VI became King of England in 1547 at the
ripe old age of nine.

NARRATOR F
And since he was so young,

NARRATOR D
And sickly,

HORATIO (*as* EDWARD VI) *sneezes then drops his shoulders*.

NARRATOR E
He had numerous advisors who helped him make decisions.

NARRATOR D
Like, what to have for dinner?

NARRATOR E
No, like how to rule the country.

NARRATOR F
It got ugly at times.

NARRATOR D
But that's not the point. The point is that as a sickly boy-king, Edward VI embraced Protestantism and enforced its tenets further.

NARRATOR E
And further.

NARRATOR D
And further.

NARRATOR F
Until he could 'further' no further. And then,

NARRATOR D, E, F
He died.

HORATIO (*as* EDWARD VI) *collapses and is dragged off by* NARRATOR B.

NARRATOR E
Thus, leaving the succession of the throne in question.

NARRATOR F
The people of England clamored for Mary!

ALL
(*chanting, as in a sporting event*) Mary! Mary! Mary!

OPHELIA (*as* MARY I) *steps forward, very happy, waves monarch-style.*

NARRATOR D
And so, in 1553, plain 'Mary' became 'Queen Mary I' – a devout Catholic.

OPHELIA
(*as* MARY I, *mutters while crossing herself Catholic style*)
In the name of the father, the son and the holy spirit, amen.

NARRATOR E
Remember, Mary was born of two Catholic parents but was shunned by her father when he divorced Catherine of Aragon.

NARRATOR F

Poor Mary.

NARRATOR E

Poor Mary, indeed.

NARRATOR D
But as Queen Mary I, she had a plan!

NARRATOR E, F

A plan…

NARRATOR D

A vision!

NARRATOR E, F
A vision…

NARRATOR D
A dream!

NARRATOR E, F
A dream…

NARRATOR D
She wanted to make England… (*rolling gesture with hand as if trying to get the others to guess the word*)

NARRATOR E
Oh! Uh…cooperative?

NARRATOR F
Snobby?

NARRATOR E
Pretentious?

NARRATOR F
Happy?

NARRATOR E
Spontaneous?

NARRATOR F
Great?

NARRATOR E
Such that no one would question her right to rule?

NARRATOR D
…<u>Catholic</u> again!

NARRATOR E, F
(*beat, then prolonged*) Ooooohh!

NARRATOR D
And so she did.

NARRATOR E
And anybody who didn't recant, dismiss Protestantism, and re-embrace Catholicism, were executed!

OPHELIA (*as* MARY I) *slashes and slashes.*

NARRATOR F
Oh, yeah. She chopped off their heads, right?

NARRATOR D
No, that's France that did all that chopping-off-the-head-guillotine stuff.

NARRATOR E
Exactly. No, Mary did not behead non-conformers. She

NARRATOR D, E, F
Burned them at the stake!

OPHELIA (*as* MARY I) *makes a poof motion with her hands.*

NARRATOR F
That's awful.

NARRATOR E
Horrible.

NARRATOR D

Well, that's what happened.

NARRATOR F
And that's how she got the nickname, 'Bloody Mary.'

OPHELIA (*as* MARY I) *has her back to the audience. She looks over her shoulder, puts a finger to her tongue then touches her hip and makes a scorching sound.*

NARRATOR E
Her nickname should have been more like, 'Fiery Mary.'

NARRATOR D
Yeah, or 'Flaming Mary.'

NARRATOR F
How 'bout, 'Turn-Me-Over-I'm-Done Mary?'

NARRATOR E
(*beat*) That's…not funny.

NARRATOR D
After burning many people for not turning back to Catholicism, Mary I died without having any children.

OPHELIA (*as* MARY I) *drops her shoulders.*

NARRATOR E
She therefore had to name a successor.

NARRATOR F
And very reluctantly, she named her half-sister, Elizabeth, as the next Queen of England.

OPHELIA (*as* MARY I) *points accusatorily to*
GERTRUDE (*as* ELIZABETH I) *who smiles
and waves.*

NARRATOR D
You see, she was reluctant to name Elizabeth successor to
the throne because Mary suspected that Elizabeth was
secretly a devout Protestant.

NARRATOR E
Which she was.

GERTRUDE (*as* ELIZABETH I) *does simple
ballet moves to fill this section.*

NARRATOR F
But Elizabeth was a shrewd diplomat. While she proclaimed
Protestantism the official religion of England, she didn't
pursue and punish as vigorously the common people who
still embraced Catholicism in the way that Mary had pursued
and punished those that chose Protestantism.

NARRATOR D
But didn't Elizabeth also burn non-conforming Catholics at
the stake?

NARRATOR F
She did, but those whom she burned were primarily men
who were openly defiant toward her and were usually men
who held offices in the Catholic Church.

NARRATOR E
You mean, old white guys?

NARRATOR F
Well…in a manner of speaking, yes.

NARRATOR E

Regarding her permissiveness with religion, she once stated,
"I will not make windows into men's souls."

> GERTRUDE (*as* ELIZABETH I) *shakes her
> head 'no.'*

NARRATOR F

Still, to make certain that religious conflicts didn't erupt, she
forbade religious drama.

NARRATOR D

And so, if playwrights weren't going to write about religious
matters, well, they had to write about something else.

NARRATOR E

Thus, setting the stage for the world's greatest playwright to
make his mark!

NARRATOR F

And who is the world's greatest playwright?

NARRATOR A, B, C, D, E, F

Shakespeare!

> NARRATOR B *jumps forward.*

ALL

In shorts!

NARRATOR B

That's why we're wearing shorts. See? Shorts. We're
wearing…(ALL *slowly turn their heads toward*
NARRATOR B *who clears his throat.*) Sorry.

> GERTRUDE (*as* ELIZABETH I) *disapproves,*

shakes her head at NARRATOR B. *Pantomime/ interpretive dance sequence ends.*

NARRATOR D
And that concludes our historical-tragical summary of the life and times of the Tudor dynasty.

NARRATOR E
You mean, tragical-historical.

NARRATOR D
Historical-tragical.

NARRATOR F
Comical, tragical-historical.

NARRATOR E
Suit yourself.

NARRATOR A
That was lovely.

NARRATOR B
Amazing.

NARRATOR C
Meh.

NARRATOR D
But that is how Shakespeare was able to write as Shakespeare.

NARRATOR G
And of course, our presentation today wouldn't be called Shakespeare in Shorts without numerous references to Shakespeare (*moans, groans from others*).

NARRATOR H

No, it's true—as English-speaking people in theatre we simply must bring up Shakespeare.

NARRATOR G

Born on or about April 23, 1564

NARRATOR H

And died on the same day, April 23

NARRATOR J

But different year

NARRATOR G

1616,

NARRATOR J

Shakespeare was the son of a glover.

NARRATOR H

And resided in Stratford-upon-Avon.

NARRATOR J

Hey, did you know that Shakespeare had three children?

NARRATOR G

(*Groucho Marx style*) No, his wife had three children; Shakespeare just helped out a little.

> *All three* NARRATORS *bend their knees quickly and stand up quickly in 'slap-stick' style while making a percussive sound with their mouths that sounds like "brrrooomp-chick!" This should get a laugh.*

NARRATOR G

(*timing is important here*)...helped out a little.

> *Again, all three bend knees, stand quickly and make the "brrrooomp-chick!" sound.*

NARRATOR G

(*timing*)...a little.

> *Again, all three bend knees, stand quickly and make the "brrrooomp-chick!" sound.*

NARRATOR J

OK, fine. His wife had three children.

NARRATOR H

Rephrase it: Shakespeare was the father of three children.

NARRATOR J

Better?

NARRATOR G

Better.

NARRATOR J

OK?

NARRATOR G

OK.

NARRATOR H

Let's move on, shall we?

NARRATOR J

OK—so, Shakespeare's wife—

NARRATOR G

(*stepping on* J's *train of thought*) Anne Hathaway.

NARRATOR J

Anne Hathaway bore three children: Susan—

NARRATOR G

the eldest.

NARRATOR J

then Judith and Hamnet both—

NARRATOR G

twins.

NARRATOR J

(*Becoming increasingly agitated at* G's *interruptions.*)
Hamnet was Shakespeare's only son and for whom one of
his most famous plays was written called—

NARRATOR G

Hamlet.

NARRATOR J

Would you cut it out!

NARRATOR H

You two should get married.

NARRATOR G

Anyway, we'd first like to demonstrate one of Shakespeare's
devices.

NARRATOR J

Can't do that.

NARRATOR G

Do what?

NARRATOR J
Demonstrate devices. (*shrugs*) It's a family show.

NARRATOR G
Sure, we can.

NARRATOR H
The way in which he wrote—

NARRATOR J
Ooooh! <u>That</u> device.

NARRATOR G
Called "verse"…

NARRATOR J
or "blank verse"…

NARRATOR G
…which has a distinct rhythm…

NARRATOR H
or musicality…

NARRATOR G
that is called…

NARRATORS G, H, J
iambic pentameter.

NARRATOR H
Performers? If you please.

NARRATOR G
Now then, iambic pentameter sounds like this:

ACTOR A

(*stressing the rhythm so that it sounds mechanical*) "But soft, what light through yonder window breaks."

                    NARRATOR H
Hey, that's Romeo's line.

                    ACTOR A
So?

                    NARRATOR H
So you're a girl!

                    ACTOR A
So?

                    NARRATOR H
So, Romeo is a boy!

                    ACTOR A
Many fine actresses have performed male-roles from Shakespeare's plays.

                    NARRATOR H
True. But, Shakespeare had men in mind when he wrote all the parts for all his plays!

                    NARRATOR G
Only men?

                    NARRATOR H
Yes.

                    NARRATOR G
In all of his plays?

                    NARRATOR H
Yes.

26

NARRATOR G
No opportunities for women?

NARRATOR H
Nope.

ACTOR B
Sounds to me like he was a chauvinistic pig!

ACTOR C
You see folks, Shakespeare used only men in his plays.

NARRATOR G
Well, Shakespeare didn't 'use' only men in his plays—men played all of the women's parts.

NARRATOR J
I'm telling you, be careful what you say—this is educational theatre.

NARRATOR H
And you're still wrong: it was the convention of the time to have only men onstage—so Shakespeare was just going with the flow of the time.

ACTOR B
So he wasn't a chauvinistic pig?

NARRATOR G
We'd like to think not.

NARRATOR H
But let's get back to iambic pentameter.

NARRATORS G, H, J
Right!

NARRATOR J

Could you repeat your line again, miss?

ACTOR A

(*again, focusing more on the rhythm than making it sound natural*) "But soft, what light through yonder window breaks."

NARRATOR H

Excellent!

NARRATOR G

And the sound of it in terms of poetry is merely, "tee-tum, tee-tum, tee-tum, tee-tum, tee-tum!"

NARRATOR H

Like a heartbeat?

NARRATOR J

Like a heartbeat.

NARRATOR G

Tee-tum, tee-tum, tee-tum, tee-tum, tee-tum!

NARRATOR J

Got it?

NARRATOR H

Got it.

NARRATORS G, H, J

Good!

NARRATOR H

Of course, no actor worth their salt would dare speak lines in so dull a fashion, focusing solely on the structure of iambic pentameter.

ACTOR A

(*offended*) Excuse me?

NARRATOR H

What I mean is, what you just spoke is the aural structure—iambic pentameter at its dullest.

ACTOR A

Well, of course—I was merely trying to make a point.

NARRATOR J

Hey, hey—look. They're not enjoying this.

NARRATORS G, H

Who?

NARRATOR J

The audience!

NARRATOR H

Well, they seem like they are.

NARRATOR J

What are you talking about? Their eyes are glazed over, a little drool is coming out of that guy's mouth, and that dude over there is asleep!

NARRATOR H

Believe me, they are definitely enjoying this!

NARRATOR J

Why 'definitely'?

NARRATOR G

Because they have to!

NARRATOR J

What do you mean, 'they have to'?

NARRATOR H

Because it's Shakespeare!

NARRATOR J

And everyone—

NARRATOR H

Whether they like it or not—

NARRATORS G, H, J

Must enjoy Shakespeare!

ACTOR B

Eh-hem. Guys? They're enjoying it because it's family out there. They have to.

NARRATOR G

Oh, don't be such a smarty-pants!

ACTOR A

You're right; this isn't funny.

NARRATOR J

Who wrote this script?

NARRATOR H

Doesn't matter. Let's just enjoy this very brief scene from one of Shakespeare's earlier works.

SCENE: *Romeo and Juliet*

ROMEO

But, soft! what light through yonder window breaks?
It is the east, and Juliet is the sun.

JULIET

Ay me!

ROMEO

She speaks yet she says nothing.
O, speak again, bright angel!

JULIET

O Romeo, Romeo! wherefore art thou Romeo?

ROMEO

[Aside] Shall I hear more, or shall I speak at this?

JULIET

'Tis but thy name that is my enemy;
Romeo, doff thy name,
And take all myself.

ROMEO

I take thee at thy word:
Call me but love, and I'll be new baptized;
Henceforth I never will be Romeo.

JULIET

What man art thou that thus bescreen'd in…

NARRATOR J

(*Interrupting the scene*.) Wait, wait, wait. "Bescreen'd"?

NARRATOR G

Bescreen'd.

NARRATOR H

Bescreen'd?

NARRATOR G

Yes!

ROMEO and JULIET

Quiet!

JULIET

What man art thou that thus bescreen'd in night
So stumblest on my counsel?

ROMEO

By a name
I know not how to tell thee who I am:
My name, dear saint, is hateful to myself,
Because it is an enemy to thee;
Had I it written, I would tear the word.

NARRATOR G

(*take focus*) That was lovely.

NARRATOR H

Brilliant.

NARRATOR J

Astounding!

ACTOR C

That was ridiculous! No woman in her right mind would
consent to a guy like that!

NARRATOR H

Doesn't matter.

NARRATOR J

Not the point.

ACTOR B

Let me get this straight: Romeo shows up underneath her window and says "I love you" and that's it?

NARRATOR G

Correct!

ACTOR A

Ridiculous!

ACTOR B

Absurd!

ACTOR C

Unheard of!

NARRATOR G

Well, they had actually seen each other beforehand.

NARRATOR J

At the Capulet's ball.

NARRATOR H

Where they share a sonnet and fall in love.

NARRATOR G

What's a sonnet?

NARRATOR J

Oh, do we have to?

NARRATOR H

(*very charming*) Shakespeare wrote 154 sonnets.

NARRATOR G
We generally concede that the first 126 are written to a man

NARRATOR J
And the remaining 28 are written to a woman

NARRATOR H
Whom scholars refer to as 'The Dark Lady of the Sonnets.'

NARRATOR G, H, J
(*in ghost like fashion*) Ooooooohh!

NARRATOR J
So, Shakespeare liked men more than women?

NARRATOR H
Possibly.

NARRATOR G
But it's more likely that Shakespeare wrote them on behalf of a gentleman so that he could give them to someone else.

NARRATOR J
The gentleman didn't write his own love poetry?

NARRATOR H
No.

NARRATOR G
But back to 'Romeo and Juliet.'

NARRATOR H
You see, Shakespeare was interested in putting the actor up against the most incredible odds and working to get them out of it!

ACTOR A

So he was stubborn?

NARRATOR H

Yes.

ACTOR B

Liked difficult situations but wouldn't ask for help?

NARRATOR H

Yes.

ACTOR C

And Shakespeare was a man, right?

NARRATOR H

Of course.

ACTOR B

See? Shakespeare was a chauvinistic pig.

NARRATOR J

Speaking of farm animals and the care of them,

NARRATOR G

Husbandry.

NARRATOR H

Shakespeare seems to have known a lot about lots of
different animals.

NARRATOR J

Especially, falconry.

NARRATOR G

How do we know he knew a lot about falconry?

NARRATOR H

Because in the remainder of the famous balcony scene between Romeo and Juliet, Juliet treats Romeo as if he were a falcon.

NARRATOR G

What do you mean?

NARRATOR H

Well, you see…

NARRATOR J

Rather than explaining, why don't we show?

NARRATOR G

But in order to do this, we'll need everyone to call out 'Juliet' loudly – as if you were playing the role of 'Nurse' and calling for Juliet to come inside – when I give a signal like this (*raises both hands in the air and makes a scooping gesture*). Got it?

NARRATOR H

Hang on. Everyone in the audience is going to play the role of 'Nurse'?

NARRATOR G

Yes.

NARRATOR H

And call out 'Juliet' when you do the scooping motion with your arms?

NARRATOR G

Yes.

NARRATOR J

Let's practice! (*goes toward audience to get them to participate*) Are we ready? (*audience may or may not respond*) I said, are we ready? (*audience should respond here*). Excellent! Let's give it a try! (*to* NARRATOR G) Give the signal! (NARRATOR G *raises both hands in the air in a scooping gesture*)

NARRATOR J and AUDIENCE

Juliet!

NARRATOR J

That wasn't so good. Try again, with feeling! (NARRATOR G *raises both hands in the air in a scooping gesture*)

NARRATOR J and AUDIENCE

Juliet!

NARRATOR J

Excellent! Once more! (NARRATOR G *raises both hands in the air in a scooping gesture*)

NARRATOR J and AUDIENCE

Juliet!

NARRATOR J

Now, you have to say 'Juliet' in the fashion that he raises his hands. So, if he makes a small gesture, you all call out a small 'Juliet.' If it's a big gesture, you all call out a big 'Juliet!' Let's try it! He's the conductor, you all are the orchestra!

> NARRATOR G *does four versions of raising his arms. One that evokes pianissimo, a second that evokes mezzo-forte, a third that evokes forte, and a fourth that evokes fortissimo.*

NARRATOR J

Brilliant! Now, let's give it a go! Aaaand, action!

JULIET

My bounty is as boundless as the sea,
My love as deep; the more I give to thee,
The more I have, for both are infinite.

(NARRATOR G *makes a pianissimo gesture,
everyone shouts, 'Juliet!'*)

JULIET

I hear some noise within; dear love, adieu!
Anon, good nurse! Sweet Montague, be true.
Stay but a little, I will come again. (JULIET *rushes off stage*)

(NARRATOR G *makes a pianissimo gesture,
everyone shouts, 'Juliet!'*)

ROMEO

O blessed, blessed night! I am afeard,
Being in night, all this is but a dream,
Too flattering-sweet to be substantial.

(JULIET *re-enters*)

JULIET

Three words, dear Romeo, and good night indeed.
If that thy bent of love be honorable,
Thy purpose marriage, send me word to-morrow.

(NARRATOR G *makes a pianissimo gesture,
everyone shouts, 'Juliet!'*)

JULIET

I come, anon. But if thou meanest not well,
I do beseech thee –

(NARRATOR G makes a mezzo-forte gesture, everyone
shouts, 'Juliet!')

JULIET

By and by, I come –
To cease thy strife, and leave me to my grief.
To-morrow will I send.

ROMEO

So thrive my soul –

(NARRATOR G *makes a mezzo-forte gesture,
everyone shouts, 'Juliet!'*)

JULIET

A thousand times good night! (*exits quickly*)

ROMEO

A thousand times the worse, to want thy light.
Love goes toward love as schoolboys from their books,
But love from love, toward school with heavy looks.

JULIET

(*re-enters*) Hist, Romeo, hist! O, for a falc'ner's voice,
To lure this tassel-gentle back again!
Romeo!

ROMEO

It is my soul that calls upon my name.
How silver-sweet sound lovers' tongues by night,
Like softest music to attending ears!

JULIET

Romeo!

ROMEO

My niesse? (*NOTE: a 'niesse' is a nestling hawk*)

JULIET

What a' clock tomorrow
Shall I send to thee?

ROMEO

By the hour of nine.

JULIET

I will not fail, 'tis twenty year till then.
I have forgot why I did call thee back.

ROMEO

Let me stand here till thou remember it.

JULIET

I shall forget, to have thee still stand there,
Rememb'ring how I love thy company.

ROMEO

And I'll still stay, to have thee still forget,
Forgetting any other home but this.

(NARRATOR G *makes a mezzo-forte gesture, everyone shouts, 'Juliet!'*)

JULIET

'Tis almost morning, I would have thee gone –
And yet no farther than a wanton's bird,
That lets it hop a little from his hand,
Like a poor prisoner in his twisted gyves,
And with a silken thread plucks it back again,

JULIET (CONT)
So loving-jealous of his liberty.

> (NARRATOR G *makes a forte gesture bigger,*
> *everyone shouts, 'Juliet!')*

ROMEO
I would I were thy bird.

JULIET
Sweet, so would I,
Yet I should kill thee with much cherishing.
Good night, good night! Parting is such sweet sorrow,
That I shall say good night till it be morrow.

> (NARRATOR G *makes a forte gesture, everyone*
> *shouts, 'Julieeeeeet!' in a prolonged fashion.*
> JULIET *exits*)

ROMEO
Sleep dwell in thine eyes, peace in thy breast!
Would I were sleep and peace, so sweet to rest!
Hence will I to my ghostly sire's close cell,
His help to crave, and my dear hap to tell.

ACTOR A
(*as commentary, to the audience*) The course of true love
never did run smooth.

ACTOR B
(*as commentary, to the audience*) What a piece of work is
man.

ACTOR C
(*as commentary, to the audience*) The lady doth protest too
much, methinks.

NARRATOR J

Bravo! Brava!

NARRATOR H

So, all those references like 'tassels' and 'twisted gyves' and 'silken thread'...?

NARRATOR G

Are all in reference to items that a falconer would use.

NARRATOR J

Right, right. And even the motions that they both make of coming together, flirting a little, parting and then repeating all that...

NARRATOR H

...have to do with how falconers train falcons to return to where they will be rewarded.

NARRATOR A

Amazing.

NARRATOR C

Brilliant.

NARRATOR B

But wasn't Shakespeare not-so-educated as other young men who actually went to advanced institutions of learning?

NARRATOR A

Indeed, sirrah.

NARRATOR B

And that is why there is a kind of questioning regarding the authorship of Shakespeare's plays. A type of conspiracy theory, if you will.

NARRATOR C

Oh, we're not going to get into this, are we?

NARRATOR A

You see, there are those even today who believe that
someone as moderately educated as Shakespeare was,
couldn't possibly have written all that is currently attributed
to him.

NARRATOR B

The conspiracy theorists might tell you that any number of
other people wrote what we call 'Shakespeare's plays.'

NARRATOR C

Among those number of people include Francis Bacon and
Ben Jonson,

NARRATOR A

Christopher Marlowe and Edward de Vere,

NARRATOR B

Even Queen Elizabeth herself have been identified as
potential authors of Shakespeare's plays.

NARRATOR C

But for now, we will refer to Shakespeare's plays as:

ALL

<u>Shakespeare's</u> plays!

NARRATOR A

All right, let's now move on to Shakespeare's mature period
in which he pondered the possibilities of the human
(*pronounce the "p" here hard for the alliteration*) psyche.

NARRATOR C

Sounds deep.

NARRATOR B

It is.

NARRATOR A

Shhh!

SCENE: *Hamlet*

HAMLET

To be, or not to be- that is the question:
The fair Ophelia!

NARRATOR C

Hey, that's not how that speech goes!

NARRATORS A *and* B

Shhh!

OPHELIA

How does your honour for this many a day?

HAMLET

Ha, ha! Are you honest?

OPHELIA

My lord?

HAMLET

Are you fair?

OPHELIA

What means your lordship?

HAMLET

That if you be honest and fair, your honesty should admit no discourse to your beauty.

OPHELIA

Could beauty, my lord, have better commerce than with honesty?

HAMLET

I did love you once.

OPHELIA

Indeed, my lord, you made me believe so.

HAMLET

Get thee to a nunnery! Where's your father?

OPHELIA

At home, my lord.

NARRATOR B

Psssst! (*the others look at* NARRATOR B, *irritated by the interruption*) Psssst!

NARRATOR C

What is it?

NARRATOR B

Ophelia's father isn't really at home. He's eavesdropping on their conversation!

NARRATOR A

So?

NARRATOR B

So, we need someone to play Ophelia's father, Polonius!

NARRATOR C

Fine. (*turns to audience*) Could we get a volunteer please?
Please? Anyone? (*to* ACTOR A) Could you help me, please?
(ACTOR A *goes into audience to choose a volunteer, brings
him or her onstage.*) Excellent. Now, hide. (*Wait for a few
moments before doing anything, then* ACTOR B *produces a
towel, puts it in the* VOLUNTEER'S *hands then lifts*
VOLUNTEER'S *hands so that she or he is 'hidden.'*) Can
we continue now, please?

NARRATOR B

Yes! By all means! Oh, but maybe go back a bit? So we can
get into the scene properly.

HAMLET

(*resuming the scene*) I did love you once.

OPHELIA

Indeed, my lord, you made me believe so.

HAMLET

Get thee to a nunnery! Where's your father?

OPHELIA

At home, my lord.

HAMLET

(*perhaps directed at* VOLUNTEER) Let the doors be shut
upon him, that he may play the fool
nowhere but in's own house.

NARRATOR B

Makes more sense now, doesn't it?

NARRATOR A, C

Shhhhh!

HAMLET
Farewell.

OPHELIA
O, help him, you sweet heavens!

ACTOR B
What's with the flighty girls in Shakespeare's plays?

NARRATOR A
She was under tremendous strain.

ACTOR A
Tremendous strain from what?

ACTOR C
From speaking Shakespeare's language.

(NARRATORS B *and* C *laugh.*)

NARRATOR A
Ah! Blasphemy!

NARRATOR B
Oh, hush up.

NARRATOR C
(*hammer the alliterations in this line*) Actually, Ophelia was just being a dutiful daughter to her padre, Polonius, while simply struggling with her hunger for Hamlet.

ACTOR A
Sounds like a personal problem on Shakespeare's part.

ACTOR B
Well, his only son's name was 'Hamnet.'

ACTOR C

'Hamnet'?

NARRATOR B

Yes, that was his name.

ACTOR A

Who would name their son 'Hamnet'?

NARRATOR A

We've already been over this.

NARRATOR C

Ah ha! Someone laughed! See, they are enjoying this!

NARRATOR B

They have to.

NARRATOR A

We've already been over this, too.

NARRATOR C

But what's all the criticism with Hamlet's inaction?

NARRATOR B

(*referring to the* NARRATORS *and addressing the fact that they are 'talking' rather than taking 'action'*) You mean like when we talk?

NARRATOR C

Yes, like when we talk and talk,

NARRATOR A

And drone on and on,

NARRATOR B

And never really do anything?

NARRATOR A, C

Yes!

NARRATOR A

Well, it's not really true that he doesn't 'do' anything. In fact, he tries mightily to ascertain the truth of his situation.

NARRATOR B

And determine if, in fact, the message of the ghost of his father is valid, credible, and believable.

NARRATOR C

For, to kill someone just because a ghost told you to do it would be heinous.

NARRATOR A

Abominable.

NARRATOR B

(*struggles to find the right word*) Wrong!

NARRATOR A

And so, Hamlet plots to determine once and for all that his uncle,

NARRATOR C

Claudius.

NARRATOR A

Did, in fact, do it.

NARRATOR B

Once he has determined this fact,

NARRATOR A

By means of the play-within-the-play,

NARRATOR C

And is later sent to England where he is meant to be executed,

NARRATOR A

Hamlet manages a number of chance-incidents that cause him to finally understand his own purpose in the play.

NARRATOR B

And what is that?

NARRATOR C

To be an instrument of Fate,

NARRATOR A

To be both minister and scourge,

NARRATOR B

And to take the opportunity when it presents itself to set things right.

NARRATOR C

In fact, it's summed up in one very famous line:

NARRATOR A, B, C

(*beat*) The readiness (*pause*) is all.

NARRATOR A

Watch as he does that very thing, here in a feat of physical dexterity…

NARRATOR B

…mental acuity…

NARRATOR C

…and blocking by our director!

HAMLET

Come on, sir.

LAERTES

Come, my lord.

> HAMLET *and* LAERTES *start to duel but are*
> *quickly interrupted.*

NARRATOR B

Wait a minute! Wait a minute! Time out!

NARRATOR C

What's the problem now?

NARRATOR B

Are we done with Ophelia's dad, Polonius?

NARRATOR C

Yes. In fact, he's actually dead at this point.

ACTOR A

(*taking the towel away from* VOLUNTEER) It's the end of
the line for you, mister/missy.

ALL

(*to a recognizable theme of doom and destruction such as*
Darth Vader's theme in Star Wars) Duhn, duhn, da-duhn,
duhn, da-duhn, da-duhn, da-duhn!

ACTOR B

Yeah, parting is such sweet sorrow and all that.

NARRATOR B

But great job! You were a wonderful Polonius! Everyone,
please, a round of applause for Polonius! (ALL *applaud.*

VOLUNTEER *is escorted back to his/her seat by* ACTOR A,
ACTOR A *returns to stage.*)

(HAMLET *and* LAERTES *duel,* HAMLET
scores a hit.)

OSRIC
Now then. Play!

HAMLET
(*they duel, then*) One.

LAERTES
No!

HAMLET
Judgment?

OSRIC
A hit, a very palpable hit.

LAERTES
Well, again.

CLAUDIUS
(*drunk*) Stay, give me drink. Hamlet, this pearl is thine,

NARRATOR C
(*to the audience*) Pssst! The pearl that the king puts into the
glass is poisoned!

CLAUDIUS
Here's to thy health! (*hiccups*) Give him the cup.

HAMLET
I'll play this bout first, set it by a while. Come.

(HAMLET *and* LAERTES *duel*, HAMLET
scores another hit.)

HAMLET
Another hit; what say you?

LAERTES
A touch, a touch, I do confess't.

CLAUDIUS
Our son shall win.

GERTRUDE
He's scant of breath.
Here, Hamlet, take my napkin, rub thy brows.
The Queen carouses to thy fortune, Hamlet.

HAMLET
Good madam!

CLAUDIUS
Gertrude, do not drink.

GERTRUDE
I will, my lord, I pray you pardon me (*drinks*).

CLAUDIUS
(*aside*) It is the pois'ned cup, it is too late.

HAMLET
I dare not drink yet, madam; by and by.

GERTRUDE
Come, let me wipe thy face.

LAERTES
My lord, I'll hit him now.

CLAUDIUS

I do not think't.

LAERTES

(*aside*) And yet it is almost against my conscience.

HAMLET

Come, for the third, Laertes, you do but dally.

LAERTES

Say you so? Come on.

(*HAMLET and LAERTES duel. No score.*)

OSRIC

Nothing, either way.

LAERTES

Have at you now! (*rushes HAMLET, cuts him across the arm*)

CLAUDIUS

Part them, they are incens'd.

HAMLET

Nay, come again. (*takes LAERTES' rapier and cuts LAERTES*)

OSRIC

Look to the Queen there ho!

HORATIO

They bleed on both sides. How is it, my lord?

OSRIC

How is't, Laertes?

LAERTES

I am justly kill'd with mine own treachery.

HAMLET

How does the Queen?

CLAUDIUS

She swoons to see them bleed.

GERTRUDE

No, no, the drink, the drink – O my dear Hamlet –
The drink, the drink! I am pois'ned. (*dies*)

HAMLET

O villainy! Ho, let the door be lock'd! Treachery! Seek it
out.

LAERTES

It is here, Hamlet. Hamlet, thou art slain.
I can no more – the King, the King's to blame.

HAMLET

The point envenom'd too!
Then, venom to thy work. (*stabs* CLAUDIUS)

ALL

Treason! Treason!

CLAUDIUS

O, yet defend me, friends, I am but hurt.

HAMLET

Here, thou incestious, murd'rous, damned Dane
Drink off this potion! (*pours poisoned wine from goblet into*
CLAUDIUS' *mouth*)
Follow my mother! (CLAUDIUS *dies*)

LAERTES

Exchange forgiveness with me, noble Hamlet.
Mine and my father's death come not upon thee,
Nor thine on me! (*dies*)

HAMLET

Heaven make thee free of it! I follow thee.
I am dead, Horatio. Report me and my cause aright
To the unsatisfied.

HORATIO

Never believe it;
I am more an antique Roman than a Dane.
Here's yet some liquor left. (*attempts to drink from the
poisoned goblet*)

HAMLET

As th' art a man,
Give me the cup. Let go! By heaven, I'll ha't!
O God, Horatio, what a wounded name,
Things standing thus unknown, shall I leave behind me!
If thou didst ever hold me in thy heart,
Absent thee from felicity a while,
And in this harsh world draw thy breath in pain
To tell my story. O, I die, Horatio,
– the rest is silence. (*dies*)

HORATIO

Now cracks a noble heart. Good night, sweet prince,
And flights of angels sing thee to thy rest!

ACTOR A

(*as commentary, to the audience*) Take note, take note, O
world! To be direct and honest is not safe.

ACTOR B

(*as commentary, to the audience*) Fair is foul and foul is fair.

ACTOR C

(*as commentary, to the audience*) Talkers are not good doers.

NARRATOR F

(*distraught, bursts into tears*) Why? Why?! Why?!!

NARRATOR D

What's the matter?

NARRATOR F

Such a colossal waste for no apparent reason!

NARRATOR E

It is unfortunate.

NARRATOR F

And now what?

NARRATOR D

Now what, what?

NARRATOR F

What happens to him now?

NARRATOR E

Well, that's exactly what much of the tragedy 'Hamlet' is all about.

NARRATOR D

What's that?

NARRATOR E

What happens next. As in, what happens when you die.

NARRATOR F

You mean, like after life and that sort of thing?

NARRATOR E

Precisely. You see, there are many questions in 'Hamlet'.

NARRATOR D

Indeed, much of the play is in the interrogative mood.

NARRATOR F

Interrogative in the sense of having or conveying the force of a question?

NARRATOR D

That is the definition, yes.

NARRATOR E

Yes, yes! What does happen when you die?

NARRATOR F

Where does one go?

NARRATOR D

Like when Hamlet says, 'The undiscovered country from whose bourn no traveller returns puzzles the will?'

NARRATOR E

Yes, that place! The place from whence no one returns!

NARRATOR F

Of course, the irony is that one person in the play has returned from that place.

NARRATOR D

Who's that?

NARRATOR F
The ghost of Hamlet's father.

NARRATOR D, E
Ooooh.

NARRATOR F
But what about the action? We were talking about Hamlet not taking action; and yet considering what we just watched, he took a lot of action!

NARRATOR E
Yes, but it took him a long time to figure things out and finally take action.

NARRATOR D
He had been sent to England where he was meant to be executed.

NARRATOR F
There were letters written by Claudius condemning him to death.

NARRATOR E
But Hamlet forged new letters and just so happened to have his father's ring in his pocket –

NARRATOR D
Which is like a way of validating a document,

NARRATOR F
And when we next see Hamlet in the play after he has escaped from pirates of all things,

NARRATOR E
He appears in a graveyard and is metaphorically,

NARRATOR D
'Bourn' of that country from which no traveller returns

NARRATOR F
So that he might finally 'set things right.'

NARRATOR E
It's really a miracle that he makes it back to Denmark alive.

NARRATOR F
It's like divine intervention, or something.

NARRATOR D
That's exactly the way Hamlet sees it!

NARRATOR E
But wait, why did Horatio want to drink the poison at the
end and die, too?

NARRATOR F
He didn't want to stick around without his best bro, Hamlet.

NARRATOR D
And Hamlet didn't want Horatio to die because Hamlet was
concerned with how he

NARRATOR F
(*for clarity*) Hamlet

NARRATOR D
would be remembered.

NARRATOR E
You see, that's all part of the 'what happens to a person when
they die' theme.

NARRATOR F

Yes, we are oftentimes concerned with our legacy after death.

NARRATOR D

Our...? Legacy...?

NARRATOR F

After death, correct.

NARRATOR E

(*beat*) Wow. I can't tell if all that's really complicated or really simple.

NARRATOR F

Definitely complicated.

NARRATOR D

Totally simple.

NARRATOR F

Definitely. Complicated.

NARRATOR D

Totally. Simple.

NARRATOR F

Complicated.

NARRATOR D

Simple.

ACTOR B

All right, all right. We've seen Shakespeare's early period, his mature period—let's move on to the tired, worn out, beaten down period.

NARRATOR F

Well, we never really consider Shakespeare 'tired,' 'worn out,' or 'beaten down.'

NARRATOR D

No, 'tired,' worn out,' and 'beaten down' are moms and dads.

NARRATOR E

Right. You see, Shakespeare applies to all generations, all times, all ages.

ACTOR C

And goes on for all hours.

ACTOR A

Would you stop that?

NARRATOR D

Yes, Shakespeare's themes and ideas pervade today's movies, plays, television, books, art, music, dance, --

NARRATOR E

and so on.

NARRATOR G

His final play—

NARRATOR H

Well, not really "final" we don't really know…

NARRATOR J

OK, then his pretty darn close to 'final' play, was *The Tempest*.

ACTOR A

Can we make this quick?

ACTOR B

Yeah, the audience is getting antsy – even if we are related.

NARRATOR G

No problem. In *The Tempest*, a featured character, Prospero, explains how he will lay his papers and pens aside and lead a simple life.

NARRATOR H

Why would he do that?

NARRATOR J

Tschhhh!!!

SCENE: *The Tempest*

PROSPERO

(*steps forward with staff and a glass of water*) How's the day?

ARIEL

Your charm so strongly works 'em
That if you now beheld them, your affections
Would become tender.

PROSPERO

Dost thou think so, spirit?

ARIEL

Mine would, sir, were I human.

NARRATOR F

Did she just say "if I were human"?

NARRATOR D

Yes.

NARRATOR E

She's a fairy and is under Prospero's spell and must do his bidding—

NARRATOR D

But he'll set her free; watch!

PROSPERO

And mine shall.
I'll break my staff and I'll drown my book. (*breaks staff, pours glass of water on his book*)

ARIEL

And so for that we here are all grateful.

PROSPERO and ARIEL bow.

ACTOR C

Wow. That was quick.

ACTOR A

(*as commentary, to the audience*) Time is the nurse and breeder of all good.

ACTOR B

(*as commentary, to the audience*) Uneasy lies the head that wears the crown.

ACTOR C

(*notices something on the downstage floor, tries to clean it*) Out, out! Out, I say! (*double take to audience, then points*) …spot!

NARRATOR D

After Shakespeare finished writing his works around 1613, he lived the rest of his life as a simple family man.

ACTOR C

Amazing!

ACTOR A

He wrote so many brilliant masterpieces all while running
his own theatre company,

ACTOR B

raising children

ACTOR A

Uh, I think his wife, Anne, did that!

ACTOR C

and writing volumes of poetry!

ACTOR A

It's absolutely overwhelming!

NARRATOR A

Well. This has all been very…edifying.

NARRATOR C

Illuminating.

NARRATOR B

Boring.

NARRATOR D

Just had to say it, didn't you?

NARRATOR B

Yep.

NARRATOR E

Couldn't resist.

NARRATOR B

Yep.

NARRATOR F

Typical.

NARRATOR B

What? What? (*to audience*) All right folks, thank you very much for your attention. We'll be passing around pencil and paper in order to have a short quiz on the life and times of Shakespeare and then you parents can take us kids out to some place for some over-priced goodie!

NARRATOR A

Pizza sounds good.

NARRATOR C

Burgers.

NARRATOR B

I'm vegetarian.

NARRATOR A

Pizza is vegetarian.

NARRATOR C

It's got cheese.

NARRATOR B

I said, 'vegetarian' not 'vegan.'

NARRATOR C

Burgers is definitely not vegetarian.

WHICHEVER PERFORMER CAN WHISTLE THE
LOUDEST
(*whistles*) Hey! Let's just say thank you and good night.

ALL *turn to audience*.

ALL
(*in unison*) Thank you and good night!

NARRATOR B
(*under the applause*) See? You two don't listen to me.

NARRATOR A
Just the two of us? Don't stop there.

NARRATOR C
Yeah, no one listens to you…

(continue ad lib)

THE END